Frontier Family

THE CAROLINE
CHAPTER BOOK COLLECTION

Adapted from the Caroline Years books
by Maria D. Wilkes
Illustrated by Doris Ettlinger

1. BROOKFIELD DAYS
2. CAROLINE & HER SISTER
3. FRONTIER FAMILY

LITTLE HOUSE

Caroline #3

Frontier Family

ADAPTED FROM THE CAROLINE YEARS BOOKS BY

Maria D. Wilkes

ILLUSTRATED BY

Doris Ettlinger

HarperTrophy®
A Division of HarperCollins Publishers

Adaptation by Heather Henson.

HarperCollins®, ®, Little House®, Harper Trophy®, and
The Caroline Years™ are trademarks of HarperCollins Publishers Inc.

Frontier Family
Text adapted from *Little Town at the Crossroads*,
text copyright 1997, HarperCollins Publishers Inc.
Illustrations by Doris Ettlinger
Illustrations copyright © 2000 by Renée Graef
Copyright © 2000 by HarperCollins Publishers

Library of Congress Cataloging-in-Publication Data
Wilkes, Maria D.
    Frontier family : adapted from the Caroline years books / by Maria D.
Wilkes ; illustrated by Doris Ettlinger.
        p.   cm. — (A Little house chapter book)
    Summary: Caroline Quiner, who grows up to be the mother of Laura Ingalls
Wilder, shares all kinds of adventures with her brothers and sisters on their
small farm in Brookfield, Wisconsin.
    ISBN 0-06-028157-X (lib. bdg.) — ISBN 0-06-442094-9 (pbk.)
    1. Ingalls, Caroline Lake Quiner—Juvenile fiction. [1. Ingalls, Caroline
Lake Quiner—Fiction. 2. Wilder, Laura Ingalls, 1867–1957—Family—
Fiction. 3. Frontier and pioneer life—Wisconsin—Fiction. 4. Brothers and
sisters—Fiction. 5. Wisconsin—Fiction.] I. Ettlinger, Doris, ill. II. Title.
III. Series.
PZ7.W648389 Fr   2000   99-41335
[Fic]—dc21

❖

First Harper Trophy edition, 2000

Contents

1.   Family Outing   1

2.   Surprise in the Berry Patch   11

3.   Critters   21

4.   January Thaw   31

5.   Cold Feet   43

6.   Circus Parade   53

7.   White Bears   60

CHAPTER 1

Family Outing

It was Independence Day, and Caroline Quiner and her family were going to town to watch the celebrations. The road was bustling with people, all headed to Brookfield dressed in their Sunday best. Boys ran through the crowd, throwing firecrackers into the air.

Zzzsss, pop! Zzzsss, bang!

The firecrackers made Caroline jump and squeal.

"Hurry, Eliza!" she cried, pulling her little sister along behind her. This was only the second time Caroline had gone to town for Independence Day. She didn't want to miss anything.

"Slow down, Caroline." Mother laughed. "The Glorious Fourth has barely begun. We'll not miss the speeches and parade no matter how slowly we walk."

Caroline sighed and fell in beside Mother and Grandma. Her big brothers, Henry and Joseph, were carrying the picnic baskets. And her big sister, Martha, was struggling to hold on to baby Thomas as he tried to toddle through the crowd.

Mr. and Mrs. Carpenter and their son, Charlie, were also on their way to town. The Carpenters were neighbors and good friends. They would all have a picnic dinner together.

It was a perfect day for the Glorious Fourth. The sun was shining and the sky

2

was a deep blue. A gentle breeze rippled across the fields of tall grass and wildflowers.

As they neared town, Mr. Carpenter told the boys to run on ahead and find a nice shady spot for their picnic. Caroline could tell that Martha wanted to go along with the boys. Martha was eight, two years older than Caroline, and liked to do everything Henry and Joseph did. And she especially liked to be around Charlie Carpenter.

When they finally reached Main Street, it was crowded and noisy. There was music playing and lots of shouting and clapping. Caroline was so excited, she wanted to shout, too. But young ladies never shouted. Caroline stayed quiet, but inside she was cheering at the top of her lungs.

Mr. Carpenter led the way as they wound through all the people. Finally, he spotted the boys under a big leafy tree near the center of town.

Mother took charge of Eliza and Thomas. She told Caroline and Martha that they were free to go play and find their friend, Anna. They could even bring Anna back to share their picnic if they liked.

"Let's find Anna fast," Martha said when they were alone. "Then we can go back and find the boys."

Caroline fell in behind Martha. Now she did not feel like hurrying. All around her people chattered and laughed. Neighbors greeted neighbors with warm handshakes and hugs. Boys tossed firecrackers into the air and gobbled handfuls of popcorn. Girls swung on tree swings and danced about

4

the square. In front of every building a cheery flag waved in the breeze. Caroline stopped every few feet to gaze around, but Martha kept pulling her along.

In front of the general store a man was reading from the Declaration of Independence. A huge crowd was standing around listening quietly. Caroline stopped to listen, too. The words made her feel proud.

But soon Martha was tugging on her arm.

"Let's go!" she whispered. "The sooner we find Anna, the sooner we can go back."

Caroline followed Martha past the shoemaker's shop and the stable. At last, she saw Anna. She and her father were standing in front of the wheelwright shop, where Anna's father worked. Caroline and

Martha had met Anna the year before, at school. Now Anna was their special friend.

"Hello, Anna! Good morning, Mr. Short," Caroline and Martha called together.

"Good morning, ladies," Mr. Short replied.

"Look what Papa made me!" Anna squealed. Her brown curls bounced as she held something out for the girls to see. It was a fife, beautifully carved out of wood.

"Be kind and share with your friends, eh darlin' Anna?" Mr. Short said with a warm smile.

"Of course, Papa."

Anna took the fife and held it to her lips. Her cheeks grew round and pink. She blew as hard as she could, and high-pitched squeaks came out.

7

"Blow softer, Anna," Mr. Short suggested. "The sound will be much prettier."

Anna tried again. This time the notes were clean and clear.

"It's perfect!" Caroline cried, clapping her hands. Then she heard a different kind of music coming down the street.

"It's time for the parade!" Mr. Short said.

Caroline turned to see a giant flag moving toward them. Its red and white stripes waved in the gentle breeze. Behind the flag marched a long line of men blowing trumpets and bugles and beating on drums.

"There are Henry and Joseph and Charlie!" Martha shouted. "There, with the drummers."

"And there are the fifes and flutes," Mr. Short said.

 8

Caroline saw children of all ages marching and skipping along beside the band.

"Go now," Mr. Short urged them. "You girls should march, too."

"I'm going with Henry and Joseph," Martha told Caroline. "You stay with Anna, and I'll meet you at the end of the parade."

Martha ran off before Caroline had a chance to answer. Anna reached for Caroline's hand, and together they dashed across the dusty street to march beside the band. All around them music blared and flags waved. The crowds on both sides of the road clapped and cheered. Anna and Caroline took turns playing the fife.

When the parade reached the center of town, Caroline saw Mother, Grandma, Thomas, Eliza, and the Carpenters standing together, waving at them. Caroline and

Anna made their way through the crowd to the picnic spot.

All the marching had made Caroline very hungry. She couldn't wait to taste the good things Mother and Grandma had packed in the picnic baskets.

After dinner she knew there would be more speeches and music and firecrackers. The Glorious Fourth was full of so much to see and do. Caroline felt proud and happy to be with her family and friends on such a wonderful day.

CHAPTER 2

Surprise in the Berry Patch

Not long after Independence Day, Caroline was still thinking about flags and fifes and firecrackers. She hummed a tune the marching band had played as she went about her morning chores. When she got back to the barn, Henry was waiting for her. He had a big grin on his face and two large baskets in his hands.

"Want to help me pick berries, little

Brownbraid?" Henry asked.

Little Brownbraid was Caroline's special nickname because she always wore her brown hair in one long braid down her back.

"What kind of berries?" Caroline asked.

"All kinds!" Henry replied. "The banks of the creek are loaded with them. I say we collect a couple of baskets before dinner and surprise Mother."

Caroline smiled and nodded. She liked giving Mother nice surprises. Especially now that Mother worked so hard.

It had been almost two years since Father's ship had gone down. Mother said Father was in heaven. Caroline missed him terribly. Grandma had come to live with them to help out, but still life was sometimes very hard around the little farm.

Henry handed Caroline one of the baskets, and together they headed off through the soft green meadow.

"We can start picking any time now," Henry said when they reached the creek.

Caroline whirled around. All along the banks, the trees and bushes were loaded with ripe, juicy berries. There were clusters of blueberries, wild raspberries, and elderberries. Chokecherries hung from the branches of small trees.

Henry immediately began to stuff his mouth with plump blueberries.

"You pick the raspberries and choke-cherries," he said. "And I'll pick the blueberries and elderberries. We don't have much time, so let's have a race. First one to fill their basket wins!"

Henry hurried off to another blueberry patch. Caroline began picking raspberries

13

as fast as she could. Her fingers soon turned purple-pink with berry juice, and a rich, syrupy smell filled the air.

Caroline wanted to win the race, so she tried hard to think of *picking* berries instead of eating them. But after a while she was putting half the berries into her mouth and half into the basket.

The berries tasted so good. She closed her eyes to savor the sweetness. Then she heard a rustling nearby and her eyes popped open.

"Henry?" she called out.

All was quiet.

"Henry?"

The rustling started up again, and Caroline whirled around. A wolf was standing only a few feet away, staring at her with big dark eyes!

"Don't move."

 14

Caroline heard Henry's voice from somewhere behind her. She knew he was too far away to help if the wolf attacked. She stood perfectly still and watched the wolf.

His fur was dark gray and his body was lean and muscular. His bushy tale was waving in the air and he was quietly panting. He did not take his eyes off Caroline.

"Easy, boy." Henry was moving closer—but so was the wolf!

Caroline began to tremble all over as she watched the wolf inch toward her, his body crouched low to the ground. Caroline wanted to turn around and run, but she couldn't. She was frozen in place. She closed her eyes so tightly, they hurt.

"Easy, boy," Henry said again.

Caroline felt something warm and sticky on her fingers. She opened her eyes and looked down.

The wolf was licking the berry juice off her fingers and wagging his tail!

"I reckon you didn't need me after all." Henry laughed, kneeling down and gently patting the wolf's gray head. "Good boy. That's a good old boy. Where did you come from, huh? Who do you belong to?"

"You don't think somebody owns him!"

 16

Caroline cried. She was still trembling all over. As long as she could remember, wolves had howled outside her window at night. She knew that wolves killed chickens, and sometimes they attacked people, too. Caroline had never heard anything about wolves being friendly.

"I imagine he belonged to somebody at one time or another," Henry said matter-of-factly. "He isn't afraid of you. Or me either."

"I never heard of anybody owning a wolf before," Caroline said. "Not even a nice one like him."

Henry looked up at her for a moment. Then he tossed his head back and laughed so hard, his whole body shook.

"So that's why you were so scared," Henry said when he could finally speak. "Silly Caroline! This isn't a wolf! He's a dog. Most likely he came to town with some folks who left without taking him along."

Caroline didn't know whether to giggle or cry. She was so relieved, she didn't even care that Henry was laughing at her.

"But he looks just like a wolf!" she said.

"He does at that," Henry nodded. "And if he follows us home and Mother lets us keep him, I think we ought to call him Wolf."

Caroline rubbed her hand along Wolf's soft fur. They hadn't had a dog for two years. Their old dog, Bones, disappeared soon after Father left for his ship. And just like Father, Bones never came back. Mother believed that Bones must have followed Father onto the ship.

"Maybe you can be our new dog,"

Henry said to Wolf in a quiet voice. Then he turned to Caroline. "Let's fill our baskets as high as we can so Mother will be extra pleased."

Caroline and Henry rushed from bush to bush. Soon, their baskets were overflowing with plump berries.

As they walked home across the meadow, Wolf stayed close to Caroline. He was still at her side when they neared the barn.

"He followed us all the way home, so he must not have any other place to go," Henry said happily. "We'll keep him in the barn until Mother says he can stay. You go on ahead, Caroline. And don't tell Mother about Wolf till I get there!"

Caroline knelt down and gave Wolf a big hug.

"I hope you'll be able to stay!" she whispered.

Wolf put his cold wet nose against Caroline's cheek. He tried to follow her as she raced to the house, but Henry held him back.

Inside the kitchen, Caroline held her basket proudly out for Mother to see.

"Goodness glory!" Mother exclaimed. "Have you ever seen so many fine berries?"

Caroline was glad to see a smile spread across Mother's whole face. She hoped Mother would be just as happy when they told her about the other surprise waiting in the barn.

CHAPTER 3

Critters

Caroline kept watching for Henry as she helped Martha set the table for dinner. She wished he would hurry up and come to the house so they could tell Mother about Wolf.

Finally, Henry came running through the door, swinging his basket of berries.

"More berries!" Mother cried in surprise. She put most of them aside for preserving, but she washed a few as a treat for after dinner.

Caroline wanted to talk about Wolf

right away. But when she caught Henry's eye, he just shook his head.

"Where's Joseph?" she asked Mother instead.

"He's still working in the garden," Mother answered. "We'll go ahead and eat, and I'll keep a plate hot for him."

Caroline could only take small bites of her beans and corn bread, she was so excited. She kept waiting for Henry to say something. When they were almost finished with dinner, Henry glanced at Caroline and took a deep breath.

"Mother, I've been thinking," he said slowly. "It seems to me that we should get us a new dog. We haven't had one around here since old Bones left almost two years ago."

Mother raised her eyebrows in surprise. "And what's made you think about getting a new dog?" she asked.

"Nothing special, ma'am," Henry fibbed. "But let's just say we found a dog, a real nice dog, and he didn't belong to anybody. Wouldn't it be all right to keep a dog like that?"

"We didn't get another dog after Bones disappeared because we couldn't feed one," Mother said. "It's hard enough keeping food on the table for all the children in this family. No sense in taking on another mouth to feed."

Mother's voice was gentle, but it was firm. Caroline let out a little sigh and looked at her brother.

"Where is the dog, Henry?" Mother asked.

"Out in the barn," Henry answered quietly.

"Where did you find him?"

23

"Down by the creek." Henry let out a laugh. "Caroline thought he was a wolf. Gave her quite a scare."

"So you've seen this dog also?" Mother turned to Caroline.

"Yes, Mother." Caroline nodded her head.

"I want to see the dog!" Eliza squealed.

"I always miss everything," Martha grumbled.

"How do you know he doesn't already have a family?" Mother asked.

"He didn't seem to have anywhere to go while we were picking berries, and he followed us all the way home," Henry said, and then he quickly added, "He's real pretty, Mother. He's gray and black and very strong, and—"

"I've heard enough," Mother said. "As

 24

soon as you finish your dinner, I want you to set that dog free. He'll find another family that can feed him and care for him better than we can."

"Yes, ma'am," Henry mumbled, looking down at his plate.

Caroline felt tears coming to her eyes, but there was no time to cry. Suddenly Joseph burst through the door. There was a terrible look on his face.

"What's the matter, Joseph?" Mother asked, jumping up from the table.

"I need you to come to the garden," Joseph answered.

"What is it?" Mother cried.

"Holes!" Joseph exclaimed. "There are holes all over the garden. And the vegetables are dying."

"It must be woodchucks," Mother said. Her voice sounded tired.

25

Everyone rushed outside. Caroline didn't see anything at first. But when she looked more closely she saw that there were big, gaping holes between the vegetable rows. Near the holes, the vegetable leaves were brown and wilting.

"Are all the vegetables lost, Mother?" Caroline asked.

"I don't know just yet," Mother said grimly. "These woodchucks dig their holes and start eating the vegetables from the bottom up. There's no telling how many plants we'll lose."

Quickly Mother told them what to do. They were to fill in all the holes with dirt. Mother, Joseph, and Henry took one side of the garden. Caroline and Martha took the other. Grandma took Eliza and Thomas back to the house so they wouldn't get in the way.

Caroline was just filling in her second hole when she heard a loud whoop.

"I got one! I got one!" Henry shouted.

Caroline stood up and saw Henry racing after a small brown creature that was scuttling out of the garden. Henry followed the woodchuck to a group of trees. Then he ran from tree to tree, searching the tall leafy branches. Suddenly he turned and rushed toward the barn.

"Where's he going now?" Martha cried.

Caroline clapped her hands together. "He's going to get Wolf!" she yelled.

In a flash Wolf bounded out from the barn door. Henry was right beside him, carrying a long stick. Wolf immediately began circling the tree trunks. When he found the right one, he leaped around the bottom, barking sharply.

Henry reached his stick into the leafy branches. The woodchuck fell from the tree with a thud. Wolf charged and grabbed it, and the woodchuck's body fell limp.

"Atta boy," Henry called, kneeling down and patting Wolf's head. "We sure fixed that critter, didn't we?"

Everyone rushed across the meadow.

When Wolf saw Caroline, he bounded up to her, his tail wagging.

"Good Wolf," Caroline said, putting her arms around him.

"Who's Wolf?" Joseph asked. "And where did he come from?"

"I don't know where he came from," Mother said. "But I think he just became our new dog."

Caroline let out a squeal of delight and hugged Wolf tighter.

"The dog stays in the barn," Mother said firmly. "And it's Henry's job to make sure he gets enough food."

"Yes, ma'am," Henry said in a solemn voice.

Martha and Joseph gathered around Wolf. They scratched behind his ears and rubbed his long nose. Mother even gave him a little pat on the head before heading back to the house.

Henry turned to Caroline and grinned.

"Guess those woodchucks are good for something after all," he said.

"I guess so." Caroline laughed. She gave Wolf another big hug.

CHAPTER 4

January Thaw

Slowly the seasons changed around the little farm in Brookfield. The warm summer faded into fall, and then winter settled in. The days grew short and cold. The snow fell and the wind howled. Sometimes the bitter wind made its way through the cracks around the windows and doors. Caroline shivered when she put on her nightclothes and when she had to leave her snug bed at sunrise.

But one January morning, something was different. Caroline opened her eyes to find the sun shining brightly through the window. When she pulled back the covers, the air was warm instead of icy cold. And when she walked barefoot to the window, there was no draft along the floorboards.

Outside, Caroline could see that most of the ice and snow had melted. And the sky overhead was a bold, endless blue.

"It's spring!" Caroline gasped. "Winter's gone! Spring is here!"

Just then Mother poked her head over the railing.

"It seems we're having a January thaw," she said with a smile. "Hurry and wake your sisters. Let's not waste a moment of this glorious day!"

Caroline shook Martha and Eliza awake. The girls dressed quickly and rushed downstairs.

At breakfast Mother said that the boys

did not have to go to school since it was such an unusual day. In Brookfield the older boys went to school in the winter so they would be free to work in the fields during the warm summer months. The girls and the younger boys went to school in the summer.

"But you all must finish your morning chores before you can play," Mother told them.

Since the boys' chores were outside, they ran out the door as soon as breakfast was over. The girls quickly helped clear the table and dry the dishes. Then they ran upstairs to tidy their room. As soon as they were through, they ran back down-stairs to find Mother.

"We've finished our chores," Caroline sang out.

"May we please go outside now?"

Martha asked.

"You may," Mother said. "But remember, you must wear your shoes and your shawls. It may feel like a warm spring day, but there's still a chill in the air. The ground will be cold and wet."

The girls nodded their heads and dashed out into the bright day. There was a cool breeze, but the sunshine felt so good. Caroline lifted her face to the sky and breathed in the sweet, fresh air.

Beside the woodpile, Joseph and Henry were busy splitting logs. Wolf was sitting nearby. When he saw Caroline, he pranced over to her, barking happily.

"We'll be finished in no time," Henry shouted to the girls. "Then how about a game of poison tag?"

Caroline and Martha and Eliza all clapped their hands. Poison tag was one of

 34

their favorite games. They hadn't been able to play it all winter long.

"Mother said we had to wear shoes," Martha said, pointing to her brothers' bare feet.

"Then wear them." Henry shrugged. "Mother didn't tell us any such thing."

"Well, if you don't have to wear any shoes, then I'm not going to either!" Martha announced.

She untied her laces and pulled off her shoes and stockings.

"It's so cold!" she squealed when her feet touched the wet ground. Then she began to dance around. "But you get used to it after a while."

Caroline looked down at her new shoes. She had been wearing them only a month, since her grandparents had sent them in a Christmas trunk all the way from

Boston. They were made of soft brown leather and had laces that climbed up the ankle.

Now the leather sides and the tip of each toe were dark with wetness from the soggy ground. The sides and soles were clumped with sticky black dirt. Caroline wanted to obey Mother. But she also wanted to keep her shoes as clean and new as possible. In a rush she bent down to untie the laces. She set the shoes on a log. Then she peeled off her scratchy wool stockings.

Shivers shot up and down her legs and spine when she stepped onto the frozen ground.

"Ouch!" she gasped.

"Don't just stand there, little Brown-braid," Henry said, laughing. "Move around some!"

 36

Caroline began to dance and hop around the woodpile with Martha.

"I want to dance, too!" Eliza shouted, pulling off her shoes and joining her sisters.

"That's some mighty fine dancing," a voice called from behind them.

They all turned to see Charlie Carpenter. He was standing with his hands on his hips, his eyes sparkling merrily. Caroline and Eliza giggled and Martha's cheeks turned pink.

Charlie offered to help Joseph and Henry split logs so they'd be done with their chores faster. Caroline and Eliza wanted to wait for the boys down by the creek. At first Martha said she would stay behind.

"But we can make grass dolls while we wait!" Caroline suggested.

Eliza clapped her hands in the air. She had never made grass dolls before.

So together the three girls made their way across the soggy meadow.

At the creek, Caroline and Martha told Eliza to wait on the bank. They lifted their skirts and waded into the ice-cold water. They began yanking big handfuls of tall grass from the marsh. When they had enough, they dunked the grass into the

38

water and pulled it out dripping wet. Then they trudged back through the thick mud.

"Where should we sit?" Caroline asked, looking around the meadow. "The ground's still awful wet."

"Let's go a little bit farther away from the creek," Martha said. "We can take off our shawls and sit on them."

"But they'll get soaked!" Caroline cried. "And full of dirt, too."

"I expect they'll get wet," Martha said matter-of-factly. "But we can set them out in the sun to dry while we're playing tag. I don't think they'll get *too* dirty."

Caroline wasn't so sure, but she took off her shawl and folded it. Carefully, she laid it on a patch of grass. Eliza sat down next to Caroline so she could see how to make a doll.

First Caroline took a handful of wet,

stringy grass and held one end tightly. She ran her other hand over the bundle, making sure the blades were stuck together and the edges were smooth. Then she looped one end over and lined it up with the other end.

"Hold this while I tie the neck," she told Eliza.

Eliza held the grass loop still. Caroline tied a single thick blade tightly around the top.

"There's the head," Caroline said. "Now for the arms."

She lifted a few blades of grass up from the left and right sides of the doll's body. Then she tied each bunch together at the tip with a blade of grass.

"And the waist," she continued. She tied another blade of grass about the middle, giving the doll a long grass skirt.

 40

"Oh, Caroline!" Eliza cried. "She's so pretty."

"She needs a necklace," Caroline decided. She told Eliza to find some berries and seeds for necklaces. When Eliza jumped up, Caroline saw that her dress was wet where she had been sitting.

"She'll dry soon enough." Martha shrugged.

Caroline felt beneath her and realized her own skirt was damp, too. Her legs were cold and tingly. She knew she should take Eliza and go back to the house, but it was so much fun sitting out in the sunshine. So she shifted to a drier spot on her shawl and reached for more grass to make another doll.

By the time Eliza came back with an apron full of berries and seeds, there were three dolls lying on the grass. They were ready for their necklaces to be strung.

Caroline and Martha were just about to show Eliza how to string the berries together when the boys came running across the field.

"We're ready!" Henry yelled. "Charlie's IT first!"

Caroline and Martha jumped up, leaving the dolls and berries and shawls lying on the ground.

Everyone gathered around. Charlie yelled, "Ready, set, go!"

Caroline ran as fast as she could through the wet grass so Charlie wouldn't catch her. She didn't think any more about being cold. It felt so good to be playing in the bright sunny meadow.

CHAPTER 5

Cold Feet

All morning long Caroline and the others raced back and forth across the field, playing poison tag. Each time a player was tagged, he had to hold on to the part of his body where he had been touched.

When Joseph was IT, he rushed after Caroline with his hand on his shoulder. Caroline squealed as she ran. Usually she was very fast. But today her heavy, wet skirts slowed her down. Joseph grabbed her by her right elbow.

"You're IT," he yelled.

Caroline placed her left hand on her right elbow.

"Ready, set, go!" she shouted. She chased after Henry until he stumbled over a clump of grass. Then she lunged forward, skidding across the ground. She caught hold of Henry's bare foot.

"You're IT!" she squealed.

"How am I supposed to catch anybody holding on to one foot?" Henry demanded.

"I got you fair and square!" Caroline giggled, pushing herself up from the ground.

Henry let out a low whistle. "You're a terrible mess, little Brownbraid," he said.

Caroline looked down at herself. Mud was smeared across her front. Clumps of wet brown grass hung from her dress and apron.

"There's a whole bunch of dirt on your face, too," Henry said.

Caroline rubbed the back of her dirty hand across her cold cheeks.

"I hope I didn't ruin my ribbon," she said. She reached behind her back and pulled her long brown braid over her shoulder.

Her precious green ribbon was gone! Mother had given it to her for her last birthday.

"Oh, Henry," Caroline whispered. She felt tears welling up in her eyes.

"Quit stalling, you two," Charlie called from across the field. "You're IT, Henry, and you have to hold on to your foot."

Henry squeezed Caroline's shoulder. "I'll help you find your ribbon soon as I finish my turn," he promised.

But Caroline didn't want to play anymore. She walked slowly across the meadow, retracing her steps.

Wolf followed close behind as Caroline looked everywhere. The ribbon wasn't in the field and it wasn't beside the dolls. It wasn't in the marsh where she and Martha had picked grass.

Caroline began to walk slowly back toward the woodpile, searching the ground. Her feet were tingly and her teeth were beginning to chatter.

"Sakes alive!"

Caroline jumped when she heard Mother's shocked voice.

"Why, Caroline, I've never seen you such a mess!"

Mother's eyes weren't smiling. Her mouth was fixed in a straight line. Caroline couldn't say a word. Hot tears began to roll silently down her cheeks.

"I found your shoes and socks," Mother continued sharply. "But where is your shawl?"

"It's out back by the creek," Caroline answered in a small voice.

"I suggest we get it immediately," Mother ordered. "Now march!"

Tears dripping from her chin, Caroline led Mother across the meadow. When the others caught sight of Mother, they all froze in place. Charlie greeted Mother politely and said he'd best be going home. He took off toward the woods.

"So you've all misplaced your shoes and socks and shawls, I see," Mother said. "Didn't I tell you to wear shoes and warm clothing?"

"Not us," Henry answered truthfully.

47

But Mother's furious glare made him look quickly down.

"I want all of you to get back to the house at once," Mother ordered. "Fetch your things and leave your wet clothes by the hearth. Then you will all to go up to bed. I'll send for you when your clothes are dry."

"We won't be able to play outside anymore?" Martha cried.

"I expect you'll spend dinnertime and most of the afternoon in your beds waiting for clean, dry clothes." Mother's voice was very stern. She took Eliza into her arms and walked quickly back to the house.

Caroline and Martha gathered their shawls and their shoes and stockings. When they reached the house, Eliza and the boys were already upstairs.

Caroline stood in front of the hearth

 48

and began to pull her heavy wet dress over her head. Her teeth were chattering. She looked at Martha, and she felt very angry.

"I should never have paid any attention to you when you took off your shoes and your shawl," she cried. "You always have to do what Joseph and Henry are doing! I ruined my dress and my apron and I have to stay in bed for the rest of the day. All because I listened to you."

"It isn't my fault," Martha shot back. "You didn't want to get your shoes all wet and dirty."

Caroline turned away from her sister. She put her head in her hands and began to sob.

"What's wrong with you?" Martha snapped. "It's just a silly dress and shawl."

"I lost my green ribbon," Caroline said

between sobs. "It was my birthday present, and it was the prettiest ribbon I ever had."

"Oh, well, if that's it, then don't waste any more tears," Martha said. "I found your ribbon under one of the grass dolls in the field. I put it in my pocket. It wasn't dirty at all."

Martha lifted her apron from the floor. She pulled the grass dolls out of one pocket and Caroline's green ribbon out of the other.

Caroline smiled through her tears. "Thank you," she whispered, taking the bow in her fingers and looking it over carefully. There was only one tiny smudge of dirt at one end.

"I'm sorry if I got us in trouble," Martha said after a little while.

"Me too," Caroline replied.

 50

"We can make necklaces for our dolls while we're waiting for our clothes to dry," Martha suggested. "I saved all the berries and a couple of long strings of grass."

Martha opened her cupped hands and showed Caroline the bright-red berries. Caroline smiled and followed her sister up the stairs.

For the rest of the sunny afternoon, Caroline and her brothers and sisters stayed inside their room. Joseph and Henry quietly told stories. Caroline and Martha showed Eliza how to string berry necklaces for their dolls.

By the time Mother carried a pile of clean, dry clothes upstairs, the sunlight was fading outside the window. But Mother didn't look so cross anymore. She smiled when they showed her their grass dolls. And she told them to hurry downstairs so they could eat their supper.

As Caroline followed the others to the table, she reached up behind her back so she could touch the end of her braid. She was sad that the sunny January day was almost over, but she was so happy that she still had her beautiful green ribbon.

CHAPTER 6

Circus Parade

The strange January thaw did not last. The weather turned bitter cold again, and soon snow covered the ground in a thick white blanket.

Just when Caroline thought that winter would never end, the weather turned warm and the snow began to melt for good. The flowers bloomed in the fields, and the trees became leafy and green once more.

Soon it was time for Caroline and Martha to go to school. Caroline loved school. It was her second year, and already she had so many new friends. She had learned all the words in her first primer and had begun her second.

One sunny afternoon, Caroline and Martha were on their way home from school. They had just reached the field near the bridge that led to town when Martha stopped. She cocked her head.

"What's that noise?" she asked Caroline.

Caroline stood still and listened, too. She heard a tinny blast, followed by a thump and a rattle.

"It's music!" Caroline cried. "And it's coming from the bridge!"

"Let's go!" Martha yelled.

The girls ran as fast as they could to the little hill overlooking the bridge. The music had stopped, but there was a line of men crossing the bridge in single file.

They wore dark blue suits and bright red hats with long feather plumes. And they each carried a musical instrument.

"It's a parade!" Caroline shouted. She remembered the Independence Day parade and wondered if she could march along to town with this band. But Martha was tugging on her sleeve.

"Look!" Martha cried, pointing toward the bend in the road.

Caroline saw two sleek black horses prancing around the corner, pulling a wide wagon behind them. Painted on the side of the wagon in bold black letters were the words: MABIE CIRCUS.

Caroline let out a little squeal. She had never seen a circus before.

"Look!" she said, pointing to two strange characters walking behind the wagon.

"Clowns!" Martha exclaimed. "I've seen them in town on posters for the circus."

One clown wore baggy gray trousers and a white shirt with red dots all over it. He had curly black hair. His face was painted white with a big red grin.

The other clown was dressed in a white shirt and colorful trousers that were stitched together from rags. His face was painted red with a big white grin.

After the clowns had crossed the bridge, the biggest man Caroline had ever seen appeared around the corner. The man's long legs were as wide as tree trunks and his boots looked as big as logs.

"He must be one of those giants Mother reads about in our storybooks," Caroline whispered.

Next came a large wooden cage on

wheels. Inside Caroline could see some kind of big white animal. Then a furry white face with black eyes and a black nose peeked out between the bars.

"It's a bear!" Martha gasped. "A white bear!"

"Whoever heard of a white bear?" Caroline wondered. In the forests near home she had seen black bears from a distance, and brown bears, too. But never had she even heard of a white bear.

"Everyone who's ever seen a circus, I guess," Martha answered.

Suddenly, Caroline heard a loud trumpet sound. She watched in amazement as a huge gray beast thumped toward the bridge in smooth rhythmic strides. It was swinging its long gray trunk and flapping its enormous ears as it walked.

"An elephant!" Caroline and Martha

shouted together.

As soon as the elephant had crossed the bridge, it lifted its long snout. It let out the loud trumpet sound again. Then it stomped off toward town with a loud *thud thud thud*.

After the elephant, Caroline watched a cage go by filled with playful monkeys and one filled with slithering snakes. She

 58

saw acrobats and beautiful women sitting on white horses.

"Let's follow the circus to town," Martha said eagerly when the last wagon rolled past.

Caroline and Martha rushed down the hill and across the bridge. They trailed the wagons all the way through town, stopping when they reached the turnoff for home.

Caroline wished she could follow the circus all the way to the next town, but she also couldn't wait to get home and tell everyone about the strange sights she and Martha had seen.

CHAPTER 7

White Bears

A few weeks after the circus parade, Caroline was walking through the woods near home gathering nuts and berries for their hog. Henry usually looked after Hog, but during the summer months, it was Caroline's job to collect his feed each evening before supper.

Caroline loved roaming through the forest with Wolf close at her heels. She liked smelling the fresh pine trees and watching the squirrels and rabbits. This evening, Caroline had taken Eliza with her.

60

Eliza dashed here and there, playing hide-and-seek among the trees and bushes.

As the shadows grew deeper, Caroline's wooden bucket became heavier. Soon it would be time to head back to the house.

Caroline was just about to call for Eliza when she heard a loud rustling nearby. She stood still and listened. There was a deep *thud* and then a strange yelp and a hoot.

Wolf began to bark excitedly. Eliza dashed out from under a tree and ran toward Caroline.

"What was that noise?" she asked in a frightened voice.

"I don't know," Caroline answered, stroking Wolf's back to calm him down. Just then another yelp sounded through the trees. Wolf stood tall, growling low in his throat.

"I saw something," Eliza whispered, pointing straight ahead. "Way down there."

Caroline peered through the shadows. Way off in the distance, she saw a white figure bound up into a tree. The next instant a second white figure followed.

"Let's hurry," Caroline said urgently. "Whatever they are, there are two of them."

Caroline grabbed Eliza's hand and began to run through the forest. Wolf followed close behind.

When the girls reached the meadow, they stopped to catch their breath. Caroline looked back toward the trees. She did not see any white figures. She checked her bucket to see how many nuts and berries had fallen out as she ran. Luckily, it was still full. She turned to check Eliza's

62

bucket and let out a gasp.

"Eliza, where is your bucket?"

"You were going so fast and the handle was digging into my fingers." Eliza's words came out in a rush. "I let go of the bucket, Caroline. Please don't be mad." Her eyes were full of tears. "We can go back and get it. We can fill it up again in no time."

"Not now we can't!" Caroline exclaimed. "I'm not going anywhere near that forest without Henry or Joseph. Those were white bears in those trees!"

"White bears?" Eliza asked, her eyes wide. "How do you know?"

"Remember the white bears we told you about in the circus parade?" Caroline asked. Eliza nodded her head. "Whatever was climbing those trees was big and fast and white. What else could it be but white bears?"

Eliza began to whimper. "I want to go home now," she wailed.

"Me too," Caroline said. She picked up her bucket and led Eliza quickly across the meadow. Wolf jogged along beside them. His ears were perked up and his eyes were alert.

When they reached the yard, Caroline told Eliza to go inside the house while she took the feed to the barn. But the more she thought about the white bears, the more scared she felt. As soon as she put the feed bucket on top of the grain bin, she rushed out the door and across the yard. She flew into the house, slamming the door shut behind her.

"For goodness' sake," Mother exclaimed. "You near frightened me out of my shoes!"

"I'm sorry, Mother," Caroline cried.

"But there are white bears running loose!"

"Caroline Lake Quiner!" Mother scolded. "You've never been one to make up such stories. What has gotten into you?"

"It's not a story, Mother," Caroline insisted. "Ask Eliza! We were in the woods and we heard some noises. There were two white bears climbing in the trees."

"Is this true, Eliza?" Mother asked.

"Yes, ma'am," Eliza said. Her eyes were big and round with fright.

Mother shook her head. "All the days I've lived in Wisconsin, I have never heard about anybody seeing a white bear." She went back to preparing supper.

"But we saw a white bear that day the circus went by," Martha piped up from across the room where she was setting the table.

"In a cage, perhaps." Mother nodded. "But there aren't any running free in the forests."

"But I saw them!" Caroline cried.

"It's almost sundown—a time when eyes can play tricks on little girls," Mother told them. "Now wash up, and not another word about white bears."

All during supper Caroline did not say one word about the white bears. But she couldn't stop thinking about them. She hardly ate a bite. That night she tossed and turned in bed, dreaming about white bears chasing after her.

In the morning Caroline crept out of bed before Martha and Eliza were awake. She knew she had to go to the forest and find Eliza's bucket. And she wanted to make sure the sun was shining brightly. She thought that white bears probably

66

slept in the early morning hours.

When she got to the barn, Henry was already there.

"Good morning, little Brownbraid," Henry called. "I was just wondering where the other bucket of feed is."

"It's still in the woods," Caroline said in a quiet voice.

"In the woods?" Henry asked.

"Eliza left it," Caroline explained. "But it wasn't her fault. We were running out of the woods as fast as we could."

"Running?" Henry asked. "What were you running from?"

Caroline's voice grew louder and her words tumbled out. "From the white bears! They got loose from the circus and were climbing some trees in the woods. We saw them and ran as fast as we could to get away."

Henry scratched his head and looked puzzled.

"But I was in the woods with Charlie last evening," he said. "And I didn't see any white bears!"

"They were there," Caroline insisted. "Two of them. They were climbing trees and making funny noises."

Henry looked thoughtful for a moment. Then the wrinkles on his forehead disappeared and his eyes lit up. He tossed his head back, yelping with laughter.

"What's so funny?" Caroline cried.

"The white bears!" Henry gulped for air. "The white bears were me and Charlie!"

"Don't tease me!" Caroline snapped. "You don't look anything like white bears!"

"Last night we did," Henry said between laughs. "We took off our shirts

 68

and trousers so we wouldn't tear them climbing trees. All we had on was our white long underwear!"

Caroline was quiet for a moment, and then she began to giggle.

"It was really you?" she asked.

Henry nodded his head and grinned. "I'm your white bear, little Brownbraid. Me and Charlie. Maybe we should join a circus!"

Now Caroline began to laugh harder.

"Don't worry about the bucket," Henry said after a little while. "I'll go get it after breakfast. I wouldn't want you to miss any of Mother's hotcakes!"

Caroline grinned. She had been so worried about the white bears and the bucket, she had forgotten all about breakfast. She knew Mother was making hotcakes, and hotcakes were her favorite.

Henry put an arm around Caroline. Together they walked back across the yard.

"I'm so hungry I could eat a whole stack of hotcakes!" Caroline said.

"I'm so hungry I could eat a bear," Henry joked, and then he winked at Caroline. "But not a white bear, of course."

"Of course!" Caroline giggled and followed her big brother back into their cozy kitchen.

Come Home to Little House!

THE ROSE
CHAPTER BOOK COLLECTION

Adapted from the Rose Years books
by Roger Lea MacBride
Illustrated by Doris Ettlinger

1. MISSOURI BOUND
2. ROSE AT ROCKY RIDGE
3. ROSE & ALVA

THE COMPLETE
LAURA CHAPTER BOOK COLLECTION

Adapted from the Little House books
by Laura Ingalls Wilder
Illustrated by Renée Graef and Doris Ettlinger

1. THE ADVENTURES OF LAURA & JACK
2. PIONEER SISTERS
3. ANIMAL ADVENTURES
4. SCHOOL DAYS
5. LAURA & NELLIE
6. FARMER BOY DAYS
7. LITTLE HOUSE FARM DAYS
8. HARD TIMES ON THE PRAIRIE
9. LITTLE HOUSE FRIENDS
10. CHRISTMAS STORIES
11. LAURA'S MA
12. LAURA'S PA
13. LAURA & MR. EDWARDS
14. LITTLE HOUSE PARTIES